AF521739

Loving God with All Your Heart

PRAYER JOURNAL

by

Susie Hobson

NORDSKOG PUBLISHING
VENTURA, CALIFORNIA

Loving God with All Your Heart
PRAYER JOURNAL

Cover Painting by Amelia Hobson

ISBN 978-0-9831957-2-6

Companion Prayer Journal to
Loving God with All Your Heart:
Keeping the Greatest Commandment in Everyday Life
by Susie Hobson
Nordskog Publishing, 2010
(Ask retailer or publisher about a discount for buying both.)

Printed in the United States of America

The Gail Grace Nordskog Collection

FROM 

NORDSKOG PUBLISHING INC.
2716 Sailor Ave., Ventura, California 93003
805-642-2070 • 805-276-5129
www.NordskogPublishing.com

This Prayer Journal Belongs To:

Deborah Westbrook

Dates:

from March 15, 2017 to ______________________

On Prayer . . .

"Real praying–that is, talking with God and maintaining communications with Him as Director of your life and activities–demands real honesty. If our prayers are to avail at all, we have to open up every corner of our hearts and minds to Him. We dare not say one thing with our lips and mean another thing in our hearts."

Peter Marshall

A Man Called Peter, "Sermons and Prayers," 1955, 337

"My chief help is prayer." "Extensive prayer is often difficult because of the weakness of the flesh, physical infirmities, and a full schedule. But no one should expect to see much good resulting from his labors if he does not spend time in prayer and meditation."

George Müller

An Autobiography of George Müller, 1899, 32

"God really does allow Himself to be moved by prayer to do what He otherwise would not have done."

Andrew Murray

With Christ in the School of Prayer, 1895, 130

"Prayer is not a lovely sedan for a sightseeing trip around the city. Prayer is a truck that goes straight to the warehouse, backs up, loads, and comes home with the goods."

John R. Rice

Prayer: Asking and Receiving, 1942, 52

PRAYERS FOR HEALING, SALVATION, RELATIONSHIPS, SPECIAL NEEDS, ETC.

Name	Date	Ans'd
Bobby Weaver	4/15	✓
Mike	4/17	
Nicki	4/2017	
Makenzie	4/2017	
Jean		
Brandon		
Norma		
Bill		
Keith		
Janet		
Wheelchr Mike		
Pastor Barb		
Jack		
Pastor Ruth		
Maryann		
Tammy		
Liz		
Holly		
Cleversburg ch		

Name	Date	Ans'd

Prayers for Healing, Salvation, Relationships, Special Needs, etc.

Name	*Date*	*Ans'd*

Name	*Date*	*Ans'd*

Prayers for Community, Church, Nation, World, etc.

Name or Event	*Date*	*Follow-up*

Name or Event	*Date*	*Follow-up*

Date 3/15/2017

"Love the Lord your God with all your heart and with all your soul and with all your mind."
Matthew 22:37

Jesus said this is the most important thing we can do as Christians:
We are to love God with everything in us.

Date

Jesus answered, "I am the way and the truth and the life.
No one comes to the Father except through Me."
John 14:6

Our belief in and love for Jesus as our Savior is the only way to have that "love God with all your heart" relationship.

Date

"This is My Son, Whom I love; with Him I am well pleased."
Matthew 3:17b

When you love people with all your heart, you naturally want to know them better and find out what makes them happy, what pleases them. Our belief in and love for Jesus pleases God.

Date

"But seek first His kingdom and His righteousness,
and all these things will be given to you as well."
Matthew 6:33

When we love God with all our hearts and seek Him first in all we do,
we lead surrendered lives—
lives that are very pleasing to God.

Date

Trust in Him at all times, O people;
pour out your hearts to Him, for God is our refuge.
Psalm 62:8

Pour out your heart to Him. We have a need and a desire within us to pour out our hearts to someone who cares and that we can trust. Trust God to hear all that is on your heart.

Date

"Behold, I stand at the door, and knock: if any man hear My voice, and open the door, I will come in to him, and will sup with him, and he with Me."
Revelation 3:20 (KJV)

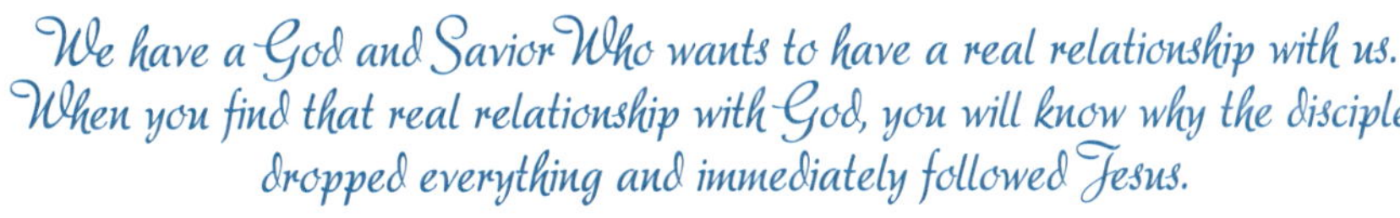
We have a God and Savior Who wants to have a real relationship with us.
When you find that real relationship with God, you will know why the disciples
dropped everything and immediately followed Jesus.

Date

"God did this so that men would seek Him and perhaps reach out for Him and find Him, though He is not far from each one of us."
Acts 17:27

If we seek to have a relationship with God, the Bible says that we will find Him. However, to seek God does require effort. The more time we spend with Him (in prayer and reading His Word), the better we are going to get to know Him and see and hear His responses.

Date

"For everyone who asks receives; he who seeks finds;
and to him who knocks, the door will be opened."
Matthew 7:8

All believers in Jesus Christ will receive, will find, and will have the door opened!—if they ask, seek, and knock.
Pursue God relentlessly everyday for He is our all in all.

Date

Jesus replied: "'Love the Lord your God with all your heart and with all your soul and with all your mind.' This is the first and greatest commandment. And the second is like it: 'Love your neighbor as yourself.'"
Matthew 22:37-39

Because God's Word is real and powerful, when we do what God says and love Him with everything we've got, obeying the second commandment simply falls into place. God wrought a change in our hearts so that we want to love our neighbor and those around us "right where they are" without all of the "if only you were . . ." thoughts.

Date

"The Spirit of the Lord is on Me, because He has anointed Me to preach good news to the poor. He has sent Me to proclaim freedom for the prisoners and recovery of sight for the blind, to release the oppressed, to proclaim the year of the Lord's favor."
Luke 4:18-19

This is the ministry of Jesus as prophesized by Isaiah and then read by Jesus in the temple at the very start of His ministry. This is our ministry, too. Spread the good news, pray for healing, pray for and help those who are having trouble and are oppressed, and provide a service that is of real help to someone. Christ has come!

Date

For all have sinned and fall short of the glory of God.
Romans 3:23

Sin is an impassable roadblock between us and God. If we have accepted Jesus as our Lord and Savior, we have a way to deal with sin: Confess and repent of it (being willing to step away from active sin in our lives). If we are not ready to do this, then we really are not ready to have a relationship with God.

Date

*"For if you forgive men when they sin against you,
your Heavenly Father will also forgive you."*
Matthew 6:14

Forgive, even when there is no earthly reason and every justification not to forgive.
God blessed us with the mercy of forgiveness even when we did nothing to deserve it.
Through Jesus Christ, we can forgive and let it go and even,
because of His love in us, pray for the best for that person.

Date

"Take My yoke upon you and learn from Me, for I am gentle and humble in heart, and you will find rest for your souls."
Matthew 11:29

God can use humble people because they are willing to go His way instead of their own. It takes strength to be humble, to step out and away from the wide road of life, and to follow God where He personally leads each of us.

Date

"This is the one I esteem:
he who is humble and contrite in spirit and trembles at My Word."
Isaiah 66:2b

These are the ones who please God: those who have read God's Word with reverence and are convicted of and broken by their sin and ready to submit and surrender themselves to Him.

Date

"I have come that they may have life,
and have it to the full."
John 10:10b

God's ways lead to liberty.
As hard as it is for our human nature to accept,
the truth is that freedom comes from surrendering our lives to God.

Date

I seek You with all my heart; do not let me stray from Your commands.
I have hidden Your Word in my heart that I might not sin against You.
Psalm 119:10–11

Because we love God we want to read His Word.
Because God loves us He gave us His Word so that we may know Him,
obey Him, and follow Him.

Date

"For I know the plans I have for you," declares the Lord, "plans to prosper you
and not to harm you, plans to give you hope and a future.
Then you will call upon Me and come and pray to Me, and I will listen to you.
You will seek Me and find Me when you seek Me with all your heart."
Jeremiah 29:11-13

*When we seek God (with all our heart) and His plan for our lives,
He is ready and willing to listen to us, answer us, and lead us
right to where He wants us to be.
God created us and has a plan for our lives that is just right for who we are, what we
are good at, what we are interested in, and where we will thrive and work the best.*

Date

Jesus asked him, "What do you want Me to do for you?"
"Lord, I want to see," he replied.
Luke 18:40–41

Just as Jesus answered and met his need when the blind man called out to Him, so Jesus is here today ready to hear our prayers and pleas for His help. Jesus is asking you right now, "What do you want Me to do for you?"

Date

From that time on Jesus began to preach,
"Repent, for the kingdom of heaven is near."
Matthew 4:17

This is Jesus' message, then and now: Change. To repent means to feel sorry for the wrongs you have done and to determine to change your mind and behavior. Dare to think of changing the way you approach life. God loves for people to change. It is rare, it is liberating, and it is Biblical.

Date

*A man with leprosy came and knelt before Him and said,
"Lord, if You are willing, You can make me clean." Jesus reached out
His hand and touched the man. "I am willing."*
Matthew 8:2-3a

Jesus is always ready to meet us right where we are today. He is never outdated.
He is not some old person whom you have to shelter from the "real world." He is prepared and ready to deal with all that is happening in our lives: the good, the bad, and even the unclean.
He is not afraid to touch us and lift us and get us going in the right direction again.
He is willing—take His hand and go His Way.

Date

Speak to one another with psalms, hymns and spiritual songs. Sing and make music in your heart to the Lord, always giving thanks to God the Father for everything, in the name of our Lord Jesus Christ.
Ephesians 5:19-20

Isn't it amazing
how singing a song of thanksgiving and praise
can make you feel so encouraged?

Date

My dear brothers, take note of this:
Everyone should be quick to listen, slow to speak and slow to become angry,
for man's anger does not bring about the righteous life that God desires.
James 1:19–20

This is such a daily discipline. The holding of the tongue must start with a resolve to hold it well before the opportunity presents itself.
Daily resolve to sift and filter thoughts to see if they even need to venture further than your mind (and then we still have to confess to idle and slanderous thinking)!
A constant challenge for believers!

Date

Whatever you do, work at it with all your heart,
as working for the Lord.
Colossians 3:23

We are called to be holy, compassionate, kind, humble, gentle, and forgiving.
Of course we fall short, yet we must get up and start right back
on the path with our Savior. We cannot afford to behave badly;
our words and ways are a constant witness of Jesus and His presence in us.

Date

Rejoice in the Lord always.
I will say it again: Rejoice!
Philippians 4:4

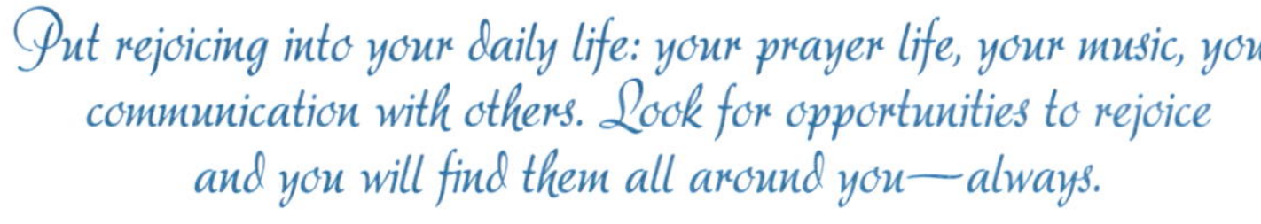

Put rejoicing into your daily life: your prayer life, your music, your communication with others. Look for opportunities to rejoice and you will find them all around you—always.

Date

I pray also that the eyes of your heart may be enlightened
in order that you may know the hope to which He has called you,
the riches of His glorious inheritance in the saints, and
His incomparably great power for us who believe.
Ephesians 1:18-19a

Dear Heavenly Father, please let us see Your incomparably mighty power at work in our lives and our families' lives today. We acknowledge that You have protected us again and again; please protect us today so that Your plans will stand in our lives. Please bless us that we will see Your incomparably great power at work in our prayer lives for our faith and encouragement so that we will know how deep and wide Your love is for us.

In Jesus' name, Amen.

Date

And we know that in all things God works for the good of those who love Him, who have been called according to His purpose.
Romans 8:28

Everything God allows to happen in your life is permitted for a purpose—and that purpose is that we will become more like Jesus.

Date

Then Jesus came to them and said, "All authority in heaven and on earth
has been given to Me. Therefore go and make disciples of all nations,
baptizing them in the name of the Father and of the Son and of the Holy Spirit,
and teaching them to obey everything I have commanded you.
And surely I am with you always, to the very end of the age."
Matthew 28:18-20

Jesus is Lord and Master of everything now and forever.

Date

"Love the Lord your God with all your heart and with all your soul and with all your mind."
Matthew 22:37

Jesus said this is the most important thing we can do as Christians:
We are to love God with everything in us.

Date

Jesus answered, "I am the way and the truth and the life.
No one comes to the Father except through Me."
John 14:6

Our belief in and love for Jesus as our Savior is the only way to have that "love God with all your heart" relationship.

Date

"This is My Son, Whom I love; with Him I am well pleased."
Matthew 3:17b

When you love people with all your heart, you naturally want to know them better and find out what makes them happy, what pleases them. Our belief in and love for Jesus pleases God.

Date

*"But seek first His kingdom and His righteousness,
and all these things will be given to you as well."*
Matthew 6:33

When we love God with all our hearts and seek Him first in all we do,
we lead surrendered lives—
lives that are very pleasing to God.

Date

Trust in Him at all times, O people;
pour out your hearts to Him, for God is our refuge.
Psalm 62:8

Pour out your heart to Him. We have a need and a desire within us to pour out our hearts to someone who cares and that we can trust. Trust God to hear all that is on your heart.

Date

"Behold, I stand at the door, and knock: if any man hear My voice, and open the door, I will come in to him, and will sup with him, and he with Me."
Revelation 3:20 (KJV)

We have a God and Savior Who wants to have a real relationship with us. When you find that real relationship with God, you will know why the disciples dropped everything and immediately followed Jesus.

Date

"God did this so that men would seek Him and perhaps reach out for Him and find Him, though He is not far from each one of us."
Acts 17:27

If we seek to have a relationship with God, the Bible says that we will find Him. However, to seek God does require effort. The more time we spend with Him (in prayer and reading His Word), the better we are going to get to know Him and see and hear His responses.

Date

"For everyone who asks receives; he who seeks finds; and to him who knocks, the door will be opened."
Matthew 7:8

All believers in Jesus Christ will receive, will find, and will have
the door opened!—if they ask, seek, and knock.
Pursue God relentlessly everyday for He is our all in all.

Date

Jesus replied: "'Love the Lord your God with all your heart and with all your soul and with all your mind.' This is the first and greatest commandment. And the second is like it: 'Love your neighbor as yourself.'"
Matthew 22:37-39

Because God's Word is real and powerful, when we do what God says and love Him with everything we've got, obeying the second commandment simply falls into place. God wrought a change in our hearts so that we want to love our neighbor and those around us "right where they are" without all of the "if only you were . . ." thoughts.

Date

"The Spirit of the Lord is on Me, because He has anointed Me to preach good news to the poor. He has sent Me to proclaim freedom for the prisoners and recovery of sight for the blind, to release the oppressed, to proclaim the year of the Lord's favor."
Luke 4:18-19

This is the ministry of Jesus as prophesized by Isaiah and then read by Jesus in the temple at the very start of His ministry. This is our ministry, too. Spread the good news, pray for healing, pray for and help those who are having trouble and are oppressed, and provide a service that is of real help to someone. Christ has come!

Date

For all have sinned and fall short of the glory of God.
Romans 3:23

Sin is an impassable roadblock between us and God. If we have accepted Jesus as our Lord and Savior, we have a way to deal with sin: Confess and repent of it (being willing to step away from active sin in our lives). If we are not ready to do this, then we really are not ready to have a relationship with God.

Date

"For if you forgive men when they sin against you,
your Heavenly Father will also forgive you."
Matthew 6:14

Forgive, even when there is no earthly reason and every justification not to forgive.
God blessed us with the mercy of forgiveness even when we did nothing to deserve it.
Through Jesus Christ, we can forgive and let it go and even,
because of His love in us, pray for the best for that person.

Date

"Take My yoke upon you and learn from Me, for I am gentle and humble in heart, and you will find rest for your souls."
Matthew 11:29

God can use humble people because they are willing to go His way instead of their own. It takes strength to be humble, to step out and away from the wide road of life, and to follow God where He personally leads each of us.

Date

"This is the one I esteem:
he who is humble and contrite in spirit and trembles at My Word."
Isaiah 66:2b

These are the ones who please God: those who have read God's Word with reverence and are convicted of and broken by their sin and ready to submit and surrender themselves to Him.

Date

*"I have come that they may have life,
and have it to the full."*
John 10:10b

God's ways lead to liberty.
As hard as it is for our human nature to accept,
the truth is that freedom comes from surrendering our lives to God.

Date

I seek You with all my heart; do not let me stray from Your commands.
I have hidden Your Word in my heart that I might not sin against You.
Psalm 119:10–11

Because we love God we want to read His Word.
Because God loves us He gave us His Word so that we may know Him, obey Him, and follow Him.

Date

"For I know the plans I have for you," declares the Lord, "plans to prosper you
and not to harm you, plans to give you hope and a future.
Then you will call upon Me and come and pray to Me, and I will listen to you.
You will seek Me and find Me when you seek Me with all your heart."
Jeremiah 29:11-13

When we seek God (with all our heart) and His plan for our lives,
He is ready and willing to listen to us, answer us, and lead us
right to where He wants us to be.
God created us and has a plan for our lives that is just right for who we are, what we are good at, what we are interested in, and where we will thrive and work the best.

Date

Jesus asked him, "What do you want Me to do for you?"
"Lord, I want to see," he replied.
Luke 18:40-41

Just as Jesus answered and met his need when the blind man called out to Him, so Jesus is here today ready to hear our prayers and pleas for His help. Jesus is asking you right now, "What do you want Me to do for you?"

Date

From that time on Jesus began to preach,
"Repent, for the kingdom of heaven is near."
Matthew 4:17

This is Jesus' message, then and now: Change. To repent means to feel sorry for the wrongs you have done and to determine to change your mind and behavior. Dare to think of changing the way you approach life. God loves for people to change. It is rare, it is liberating, and it is Biblical.

Date

A man with leprosy came and knelt before Him and said,
"Lord, if You are willing, You can make me clean." Jesus reached out
His hand and touched the man. "I am willing."
Matthew 8:2–3a

Jesus is always ready to meet us right where we are today. He is never outdated. He is not some old person whom you have to shelter from the "real world." He is prepared and ready to deal with all that is happening in our lives: the good, the bad, and even the unclean. He is not afraid to touch us and lift us and get us going in the right direction again. He is willing—take His hand and go His Way.

Date

Speak to one another with psalms, hymns and spiritual songs. Sing and make music in your heart to the Lord, always giving thanks to God the Father for everything, in the name of our Lord Jesus Christ.

Ephesians 5:19–20

Isn't it amazing
how singing a song of thanksgiving and praise
can make you feel so encouraged?

Date

My dear brothers, take note of this:
Everyone should be quick to listen, slow to speak and slow to become angry,
for man's anger does not bring about the righteous life that God desires.
James 1:19-20

This is such a daily discipline. The holding of the tongue must start with
a resolve to hold it well before the opportunity presents itself.
Daily resolve to sift and filter thoughts to see if they even need to venture further
than your mind (and then we still have to confess to idle and slanderous thinking)!
A constant challenge for believers!

Date

Whatever you do, work at it with all your heart,
as working for the Lord.
Colossians 3:23

We are called to be holy, compassionate, kind, humble, gentle, and forgiving.
Of course we fall short, yet we must get up and start right back
on the path with our Savior. We cannot afford to behave badly;
our words and ways are a constant witness of Jesus and His presence in us.

Date

Rejoice in the Lord always.
I will say it again: Rejoice!
Philippians 4:4

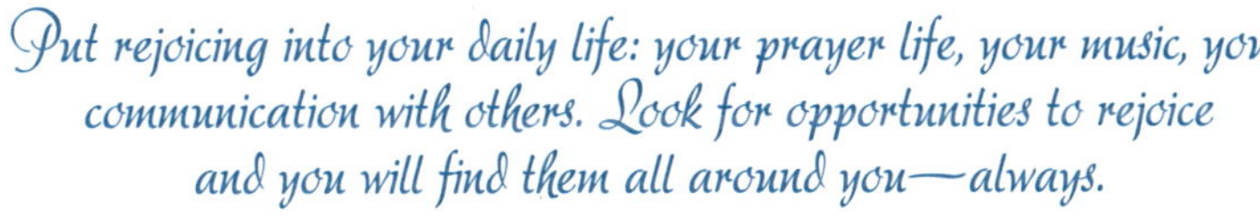
Put rejoicing into your daily life: your prayer life, your music, your communication with others. Look for opportunities to rejoice and you will find them all around you—always.

Date

I pray also that the eyes of your heart may be enlightened
in order that you may know the hope to which He has called you,
the riches of His glorious inheritance in the saints, and
His incomparably great power for us who believe.
Ephesians 1:18–19a

Dear Heavenly Father, please let us see Your incomparably mighty power at work in our lives and our families' lives today. We acknowledge that You have protected us again and again; please protect us today so that Your plans will stand in our lives. Please bless us that we will see Your incomparably great power at work in our prayer lives for our faith and encouragement so that we will know how deep and wide Your love is for us.
In Jesus' name, Amen.

Date

And we know that in all things God works for the good of those who love Him,
who have been called according to His purpose.
Romans 8:28

Everything God allows to happen in your life is permitted for a purpose—and that purpose is that we will become more like Jesus.

Date

Then Jesus came to them and said, "All authority in heaven and on earth
has been given to Me. Therefore go and make disciples of all nations,
baptizing them in the name of the Father and of the Son and of the Holy Spirit,
and teaching them to obey everything I have commanded you.
And surely I am with you always, to the very end of the age."
Matthew 28:18-20

Jesus is Lord and Master of everything now and forever.

Date

"Love the Lord your God with all your heart and with all your soul and with all your mind."
Matthew 22:37

Jesus said this is the most important thing we can do as Christians:
We are to love God with everything in us.

Date

Jesus answered, "I am the way and the truth and the life.
No one comes to the Father except through Me."
John 14:6

Our belief in and love for Jesus as our Savior is the only way to have that "love God with all your heart" relationship.

Date

"This is My Son, Whom I love; with Him I am well pleased."
Matthew 3:17b

When you love people with all your heart, you naturally want to know them better and find out what makes them happy, what pleases them. Our belief in and love for Jesus pleases God.

Date

"But seek first His kingdom and His righteousness,
and all these things will be given to you as well."
Matthew 6:33

When we love God with all our hearts and seek Him first in all we do,
we lead surrendered lives—
lives that are very pleasing to God.

Date

Trust in Him at all times, O people;
pour out your hearts to Him, for God is our refuge.
Psalm 62:8

Pour out your heart to Him. We have a need and a desire within us to pour out our hearts to someone who cares and that we can trust. Trust God to hear all that is on your heart.

Date

"Behold, I stand at the door, and knock: if any man hear My voice, and open the door, I will come in to him, and will sup with him, and he with Me."
Revelation 3:20 (KJV)

We have a God and Savior Who wants to have a real relationship with us. When you find that real relationship with God, you will know why the disciples dropped everything and immediately followed Jesus.

Date

"God did this so that men would seek Him and perhaps reach out for Him and find Him, though He is not far from each one of us."

Acts 17:27

If we seek to have a relationship with God, the Bible says that we will find Him. However, to seek God does require effort. The more time we spend with Him (in prayer and reading His Word), the better we are going to get to know Him and see and hear His responses.

Date

"For everyone who asks receives; he who seeks finds; and to him who knocks, the door will be opened."
Matthew 7:8

All believers in Jesus Christ will receive, will find, and will have the door opened!—if they ask, seek, and knock. Pursue God relentlessly everyday for He is our all in all.

Date

Jesus replied: "'Love the Lord your God with all your heart and with all your soul and with all your mind.' This is the first and greatest commandment. And the second is like it: 'Love your neighbor as yourself.'"
Matthew 22:37-39

Because God's Word is real and powerful, when we do what God says and love Him with everything we've got, obeying the second commandment simply falls into place. God wrought a change in our hearts so that we want to love our neighbor and those around us "right where they are" without all of the "if only you were . . ." thoughts.

Date

"The Spirit of the Lord is on Me, because He has anointed Me to preach good news to the poor. He has sent Me to proclaim freedom for the prisoners and recovery of sight for the blind, to release the oppressed, to proclaim the year of the Lord's favor."
Luke 4:18–19

This is the ministry of Jesus as prophesized by Isaiah and then read by Jesus in the temple at the very start of His ministry. This is our ministry, too. Spread the good news, pray for healing, pray for and help those who are having trouble and are oppressed, and provide a service that is of real help to someone. Christ has come!

Date

For all have sinned and fall short of the glory of God.
Romans 3:23

Sin is an impassable roadblock between us and God. If we have accepted Jesus as our Lord and Savior, we have a way to deal with sin: Confess and repent of it (being willing to step away from active sin in our lives). If we are not ready to do this, then we really are not ready to have a relationship with God.

Date

"For if you forgive men when they sin against you,
your Heavenly Father will also forgive you."
Matthew 6:14

Forgive, even when there is no earthly reason and every justification not to forgive.
God blessed us with the mercy of forgiveness even when we did nothing to deserve it.
Through Jesus Christ, we can forgive and let it go and even,
because of His love in us, pray for the best for that person.

Date

"Take My yoke upon you and learn from Me, for I am gentle and humble in heart, and you will find rest for your souls."
Matthew 11:29

God can use humble people because they are willing to go His way instead of their own. It takes strength to be humble, to step out and away from the wide road of life, and to follow God where He personally leads each of us.

Date

"This is the one I esteem:
he who is humble and contrite in spirit and trembles at My Word."
Isaiah 66:2b

These are the ones who please God: those who have read God's Word with reverence and are convicted of and broken by their sin and ready to submit and surrender themselves to Him.

Date

"I have come that they may have life,
and have it to the full."
John 10:10b

God's ways lead to liberty.
As hard as it is for our human nature to accept,
the truth is that freedom comes from surrendering our lives to God.

Date

I seek You with all my heart; do not let me stray from Your commands.
I have hidden Your Word in my heart that I might not sin against You.
Psalm 119:10-11

Because we love God we want to read His Word.
Because God loves us He gave us His Word so that we may know Him,
obey Him, and follow Him.

Date

"For I know the plans I have for you," declares the Lord, "plans to prosper you
and not to harm you, plans to give you hope and a future.
Then you will call upon Me and come and pray to Me, and I will listen to you.
You will seek Me and find Me when you seek Me with all your heart."
Jeremiah 29:11-13

When we seek God (with all our heart) and His plan for our lives,
He is ready and willing to listen to us, answer us, and lead us
right to where He wants us to be.
God created us and has a plan for our lives that is just right for who we are, what we are good at, what we are interested in, and where we will thrive and work the best.

Date

Jesus asked him, "What do you want Me to do for you?"
"Lord, I want to see," he replied.
Luke 18:40–41

Just as Jesus answered and met his need when the blind man called out to Him, so Jesus is here today ready to hear our prayers and pleas for His help. Jesus is asking you right now, "What do you want Me to do for you?"

Date

From that time on Jesus began to preach,
"Repent, for the kingdom of heaven is near."
Matthew 4:17

This is Jesus' message, then and now: Change. To repent means to feel sorry for the wrongs you have done and to determine to change your mind and behavior. Dare to think of changing the way you approach life. God loves for people to change. It is rare, it is liberating, and it is Biblical.

Date

A man with leprosy came and knelt before Him and said,
"Lord, if You are willing, You can make me clean." Jesus reached out
His hand and touched the man. "I am willing."
Matthew 8:2–3a

Jesus is always ready to meet us right where we are today. He is never outdated.
He is not some old person whom you have to shelter from the "real world." He is prepared and ready to deal with all that is happening in our lives: the good, the bad, and even the unclean. He is not afraid to touch us and lift us and get us going in the right direction again.
He is willing—take His hand and go His Way.

Date

Speak to one another with psalms, hymns and spiritual songs. Sing and make music in your heart to the Lord, always giving thanks to God the Father for everything, in the name of our Lord Jesus Christ.
Ephesians 5:19–20

*Isn't it amazing
how singing a song of thanksgiving and praise
can make you feel so encouraged?*

Date

My dear brothers, take note of this:
Everyone should be quick to listen, slow to speak and slow to become angry,
for man's anger does not bring about the righteous life that God desires.
James 1:19–20

This is such a daily discipline. The holding of the tongue must start with a resolve to hold it well before the opportunity presents itself. Daily resolve to sift and filter thoughts to see if they even need to venture further than your mind (and then we still have to confess to idle and slanderous thinking)! A constant challenge for believers!

Date

Whatever you do, work at it with all your heart,
as working for the Lord.
Colossians 3:23

We are called to be holy, compassionate, kind, humble, gentle, and forgiving.
Of course we fall short, yet we must get up and start right back
on the path with our Savior. We cannot afford to behave badly;
our words and ways are a constant witness of Jesus and His presence in us.

Date

Rejoice in the Lord always.
I will say it again: Rejoice!
Philippians 4:4

Put rejoicing into your daily life: your prayer life, your music, your communication with others. Look for opportunities to rejoice and you will find them all around you—always.

Date

*I pray also that the eyes of your heart may be enlightened
in order that you may know the hope to which He has called you,
the riches of His glorious inheritance in the saints, and
His incomparably great power for us who believe.*
Ephesians 1:18–19a

Dear Heavenly Father, please let us see Your incomparably mighty power at work in our lives and our families' lives today. We acknowledge that You have protected us again and again; please protect us today so that Your plans will stand in our lives. Please bless us that we will see Your incomparably great power at work in our prayer lives for our faith and encouragement so that we will know how deep and wide Your love is for us.
In Jesus' name, Amen.

Date

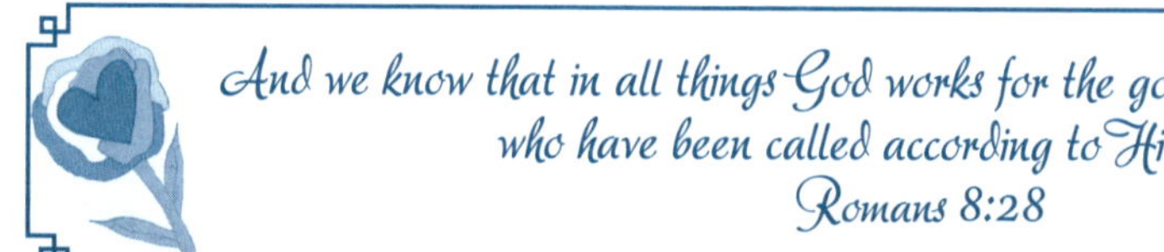

And we know that in all things God works for the good of those who love Him, who have been called according to His purpose.
Romans 8:28

Everything God allows to happen in your life is permitted for a purpose—and that purpose is that we will become more like Jesus.

Date

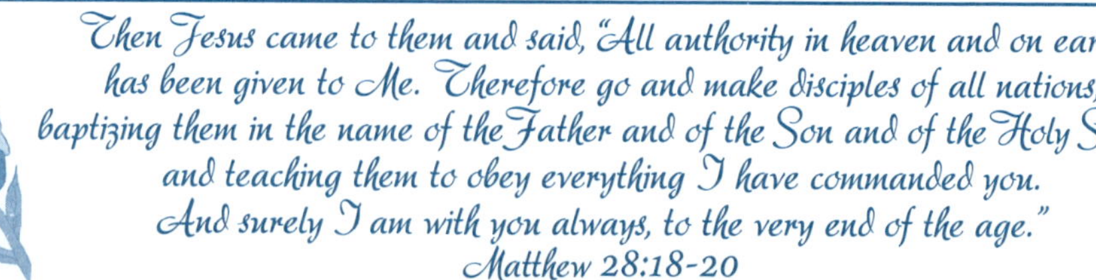

Then Jesus came to them and said, "All authority in heaven and on earth has been given to Me. Therefore go and make disciples of all nations, baptizing them in the name of the Father and of the Son and of the Holy Spirit, and teaching them to obey everything I have commanded you. And surely I am with you always, to the very end of the age."

Matthew 28:18-20

Jesus is Lord and Master of everything now and forever.

Date

"Love the Lord your God with all your heart and
with all your soul and with all your mind."
Matthew 22:37

Jesus said this is the most important thing we can do as Christians:
We are to love God with everything in us.

Date

Jesus answered, "I am the way and the truth and the life.
No one comes to the Father except through Me."
John 14:6

Our belief in and love for Jesus as our Savior is the only way to have that "love God with all your heart" relationship.

Date

"This is My Son, Whom I love; with Him I am well pleased."
Matthew 3:17b

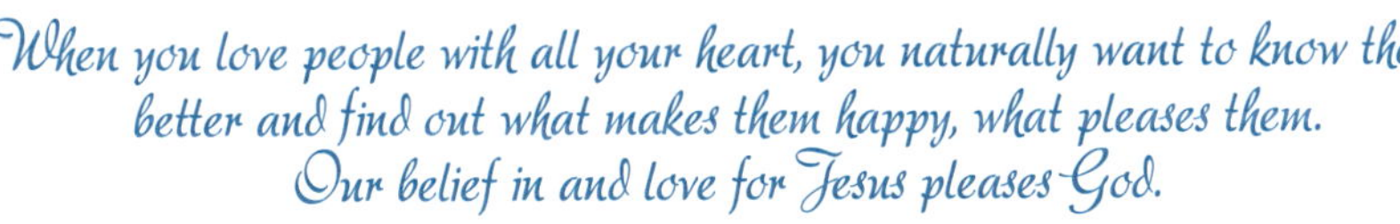
When you love people with all your heart, you naturally want to know them
better and find out what makes them happy, what pleases them.
Our belief in and love for Jesus pleases God.

Date

"But seek first His kingdom and His righteousness,
and all these things will be given to you as well."
Matthew 6:33

When we love God with all our hearts and seek Him first in all we do,
we lead surrendered lives—
lives that are very pleasing to God.

Date

Trust in Him at all times, O people;
pour out your hearts to Him, for God is our refuge.
Psalm 62:8

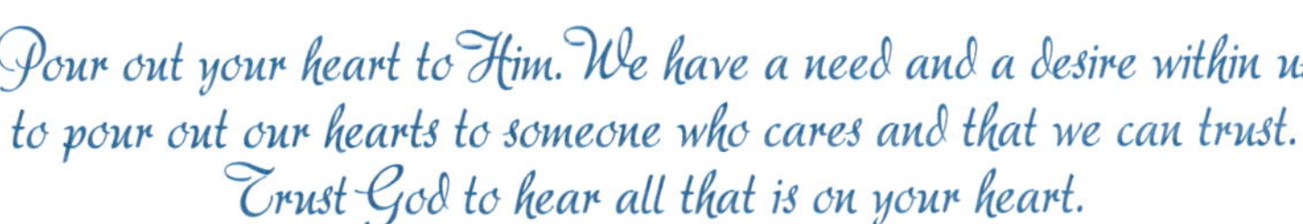
Pour out your heart to Him. We have a need and a desire within us
to pour out our hearts to someone who cares and that we can trust.
Trust God to hear all that is on your heart.

Date

"Behold, I stand at the door, and knock: if any man hear My voice, and open the door, I will come in to him, and will sup with him, and he with Me."

Revelation 3:20 (KJV)

We have a God and Savior Who wants to have a real relationship with us. When you find that real relationship with God, you will know why the disciples dropped everything and immediately followed Jesus.

Date

"God did this so that men would seek Him and perhaps reach out for Him
and find Him, though He is not far from each one of us."
Acts 17:27

If we seek to have a relationship with God, the Bible says that we will find Him. However, to seek God does require effort. The more time we spend with Him (in prayer and reading His Word), the better we are going to get to know Him and see and hear His responses.

Date

"For everyone who asks receives; he who seeks finds; and to him who knocks, the door will be opened."
Matthew 7:8

All believers in Jesus Christ will receive, will find, and will have the door opened!—if they ask, seek, and knock. Pursue God relentlessly everyday for He is our all in all.

Date

Jesus replied: "'Love the Lord your God with all your heart and with all your
soul and with all your mind.' This is the first and greatest commandment.
And the second is like it: 'Love your neighbor as yourself.'"
Matthew 22:37-39

Because God's Word is real and powerful, when we do what God says and love Him with everything we've got, obeying the second commandment simply falls into place. God wrought a change in our hearts so that we want to love our neighbor and those around us "right where they are" without all of the "if only you were . . ." thoughts.

Date

"The Spirit of the Lord is on Me, because He has anointed Me to preach good news to the poor. He has sent Me to proclaim freedom for the prisoners and recovery of sight for the blind, to release the oppressed, to proclaim the year of the Lord's favor."
Luke 4:18–19

This is the ministry of Jesus as prophesized by Isaiah and then read by Jesus in the temple at the very start of His ministry. This is our ministry, too. Spread the good news, pray for healing, pray for and help those who are having trouble and are oppressed, and provide a service that is of real help to someone. Christ has come!

Date

For all have sinned and fall short of the glory of God.
Romans 3:23

Sin is an impassable roadblock between us and God. If we have accepted Jesus as our Lord and Savior, we have a way to deal with sin: Confess and repent of it (being willing to step away from active sin in our lives). If we are not ready to do this, then we really are not ready to have a relationship with God.

Date

*"For if you forgive men when they sin against you,
your Heavenly Father will also forgive you."*
Matthew 6:14

Forgive, even when there is no earthly reason and every justification not to forgive.
God blessed us with the mercy of forgiveness even when we did nothing to deserve it.
Through Jesus Christ, we can forgive and let it go and even,
because of His love in us, pray for the best for that person.

Date

"Take My yoke upon you and learn from Me, for I am gentle and humble in heart, and you will find rest for your souls."
Matthew 11:29

God can use humble people because they are willing to go His way instead of their own. It takes strength to be humble, to step out and away from the wide road of life, and to follow God where He personally leads each of us.

Date

"This is the one I esteem:
he who is humble and contrite in spirit and trembles at My Word."
Isaiah 66:2b

These are the ones who please God: those who have read God's Word with reverence and are convicted of and broken by their sin and ready to submit and surrender themselves to Him.

Date

"I have come that they may have life,
and have it to the full."
John 10:10b

God's ways lead to liberty.
As hard as it is for our human nature to accept,
the truth is that freedom comes from surrendering our lives to God.

Date

I seek You with all my heart; do not let me stray from Your commands.
I have hidden Your Word in my heart that I might not sin against You.
Psalm 119:10–11

Because we love God we want to read His Word.
Because God loves us He gave us His Word so that we may know Him, obey Him, and follow Him.

Date

"For I know the plans I have for you," declares the Lord, "plans to prosper you
and not to harm you, plans to give you hope and a future.
Then you will call upon Me and come and pray to Me, and I will listen to you.
You will seek Me and find Me when you seek Me with all your heart."
Jeremiah 29:11-13

When we seek God (with all our heart) and His plan for our lives,
He is ready and willing to listen to us, answer us, and lead us
right to where He wants us to be.

God created us and has a plan for our lives that is just right for who we are, what we are good at, what we are interested in, and where we will thrive and work the best.

Date

Jesus asked him, "What do you want Me to do for you?"
"Lord, I want to see," he replied.
Luke 18:40-41

Just as Jesus answered and met his need when the blind man called out to Him, so Jesus is here today ready to hear our prayers and pleas for His help. Jesus is asking you right now, "What do you want Me to do for you?"

Date

From that time on Jesus began to preach,
"Repent, for the kingdom of heaven is near."
Matthew 4:17

This is Jesus' message, then and now: Change. To repent means to feel sorry for the wrongs you have done and to determine to change your mind and behavior. Dare to think of changing the way you approach life. God loves for people to change. It is rare, it is liberating, and it is Biblical.

Date

*A man with leprosy came and knelt before Him and said,
"Lord, if You are willing, You can make me clean." Jesus reached out
His hand and touched the man. "I am willing."
Matthew 8:2–3a*

Jesus is always ready to meet us right where we are today. He is never outdated. He is not some old person whom you have to shelter from the "real world." He is prepared and ready to deal with all that is happening in our lives: the good, the bad, and even the unclean. He is not afraid to touch us and lift us and get us going in the right direction again. He is willing—take His hand and go His Way.

Date

Speak to one another with psalms, hymns and spiritual songs. Sing and make music in your heart to the Lord, always giving thanks to God the Father for everything, in the name of our Lord Jesus Christ.

Ephesians 5:19-20

Isn't it amazing
how singing a song of thanksgiving and praise
can make you feel so encouraged?

Date

My dear brothers, take note of this:
Everyone should be quick to listen, slow to speak and slow to become angry,
for man's anger does not bring about the righteous life that God desires.
James 1:19–20

This is such a daily discipline. The holding of the tongue must start with a resolve to hold it well before the opportunity presents itself. Daily resolve to sift and filter thoughts to see if they even need to venture further than your mind (and then we still have to confess to idle and slanderous thinking)! A constant challenge for believers!

Date

Whatever you do, work at it with all your heart,
as working for the Lord.
Colossians 3:23

We are called to be holy, compassionate, kind, humble, gentle, and forgiving.
Of course we fall short, yet we must get up and start right back
on the path with our Savior. We cannot afford to behave badly;
our words and ways are a constant witness of Jesus and His presence in us.

Date

Rejoice in the Lord always.
I will say it again: Rejoice!
Philippians 4:4

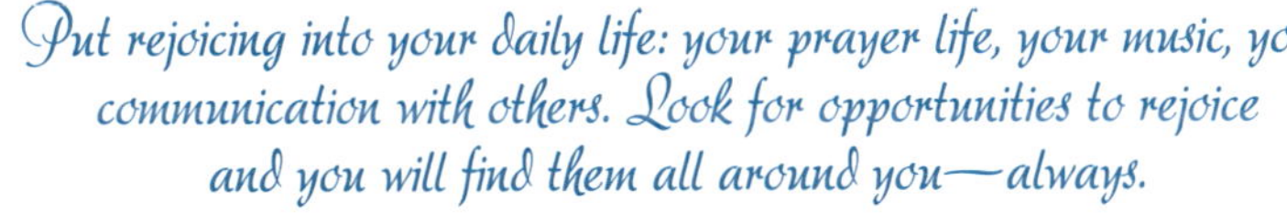

Put rejoicing into your daily life: your prayer life, your music, your communication with others. Look for opportunities to rejoice and you will find them all around you—always.

Date

*I pray also that the eyes of your heart may be enlightened
in order that you may know the hope to which He has called you,
the riches of His glorious inheritance in the saints, and
His incomparably great power for us who believe.*
Ephesians 1:18–19a

Dear Heavenly Father, please let us see Your incomparably mighty power at work in our lives and our families' lives today. We acknowledge that You have protected us again and again; please protect us today so that Your plans will stand in our lives. Please bless us that we will see Your incomparably great power at work in our prayer lives for our faith and encouragement so that we will know how deep and wide Your love is for us.

In Jesus' name, Amen.

Date

And we know that in all things God works for the good of those who love Him, who have been called according to His purpose.
Romans 8:28

Everything God allows to happen in your life is permitted for a purpose—and that purpose is that we will become more like Jesus.

Date

Then Jesus came to them and said, "All authority in heaven and on earth has been given to Me. Therefore go and make disciples of all nations, baptizing them in the name of the Father and of the Son and of the Holy Spirit, and teaching them to obey everything I have commanded you. And surely I am with you always, to the very end of the age."
Matthew 28:18-20

Jesus is Lord and Master of everything now and forever.

Date

"Love the Lord your God with all your heart and
with all your soul and with all your mind."
Matthew 22:37

Jesus said this is the most important thing we can do as Christians:
We are to love God with everything in us.

Date

Jesus answered, "I am the way and the truth and the life. No one comes to the Father except through Me."
John 14:6

Our belief in and love for Jesus as our Savior is the only way to have that "love God with all your heart" relationship.

Date

"This is My Son, Whom I love; with Him I am well pleased."
Matthew 3:17b

When you love people with all your heart, you naturally want to know them better and find out what makes them happy, what pleases them. Our belief in and love for Jesus pleases God.

Date

"But seek first His kingdom and His righteousness,
and all these things will be given to you as well."
Matthew 6:33

When we love God with all our hearts and seek Him first in all we do,
we lead surrendered lives—
lives that are very pleasing to God.

Date

Trust in Him at all times, O people;
pour out your hearts to Him, for God is our refuge.
Psalm 62:8

Pour out your heart to Him. We have a need and a desire within us to pour out our hearts to someone who cares and that we can trust. Trust God to hear all that is on your heart.

Date

"Behold, I stand at the door, and knock: if any man hear My voice, and open the door, I will come in to him, and will sup with him, and he with Me."
Revelation 3:20 (KJV)

We have a God and Savior Who wants to have a real relationship with us. When you find that real relationship with God, you will know why the disciples dropped everything and immediately followed Jesus.

Date

"God did this so that men would seek Him and perhaps reach out for Him and find Him, though He is not far from each one of us."
Acts 17:27

If we seek to have a relationship with God, the Bible says that we will find Him. However, to seek God does require effort. The more time we spend with Him (in prayer and reading His Word), the better we are going to get to know Him and see and hear His responses.

Date

"For everyone who asks receives; he who seeks finds;
and to him who knocks, the door will be opened."
Matthew 7:8

All believers in Jesus Christ will receive, will find, and will have
the door opened!—if they ask, seek, and knock.
Pursue God relentlessly everyday for He is our all in all.

Date

Jesus replied: "'Love the Lord your God with all your heart and with all your soul and with all your mind.' This is the first and greatest commandment. And the second is like it: 'Love your neighbor as yourself.'"
Matthew 22:37-39

Because God's Word is real and powerful, when we do what God says and love Him with everything we've got, obeying the second commandment simply falls into place. God wrought a change in our hearts so that we want to love our neighbor and those around us "right where they are" without all of the "if only you were . . ." thoughts.

Date

"The Spirit of the Lord is on Me, because He has anointed Me to preach good news to the poor. He has sent Me to proclaim freedom for the prisoners and recovery of sight for the blind, to release the oppressed, to proclaim the year of the Lord's favor."
Luke 4:18–19

This is the ministry of Jesus as prophesized by Isaiah and then read by Jesus in the temple at the very start of His ministry. This is our ministry, too. Spread the good news, pray for healing, pray for and help those who are having trouble and are oppressed, and provide a service that is of real help to someone. Christ has come!

Date

For all have sinned and fall short of the glory of God.
Romans 3:23

Sin is an impassable roadblock between us and God. If we have accepted Jesus as our Lord and Savior, we have a way to deal with sin: Confess and repent of it (being willing to step away from active sin in our lives). If we are not ready to do this, then we really are not ready to have a relationship with God.

Date

"For if you forgive men when they sin against you,
your Heavenly Father will also forgive you."
Matthew 6:14

Forgive, even when there is no earthly reason and every justification not to forgive.
God blessed us with the mercy of forgiveness even when we did nothing to deserve it.
Through Jesus Christ, we can forgive and let it go and even,
because of His love in us, pray for the best for that person.

Date

"Take My yoke upon you and learn from Me, for I am gentle and humble in heart, and you will find rest for your souls."
Matthew 11:29

God can use humble people because they are willing to go His way instead of their own. It takes strength to be humble, to step out and away from the wide road of life, and to follow God where He personally leads each of us.

Date

"This is the one I esteem:
he who is humble and contrite in spirit and trembles at My Word."
Isaiah 66:2b

These are the ones who please God: those who have read God's Word with reverence and are convicted of and broken by their sin and ready to submit and surrender themselves to Him.

Date

"I have come that they may have life,
and have it to the full."
John 10:10b

God's ways lead to liberty.
As hard as it is for our human nature to accept,
the truth is that freedom comes from surrendering our lives to God.

Date

I seek You with all my heart; do not let me stray from Your commands.
I have hidden Your Word in my heart that I might not sin against You.
Psalm 119:10-11

Because we love God we want to read His Word.
Because God loves us He gave us His Word so that we may know Him,
obey Him, and follow Him.

Date

"For I know the plans I have for you," declares the Lord, "plans to prosper you
and not to harm you, plans to give you hope and a future.
Then you will call upon Me and come and pray to Me, and I will listen to you.
You will seek Me and find Me when you seek Me with all your heart."
Jeremiah 29:11-13

When we seek God (with all our heart) and His plan for our lives,
He is ready and willing to listen to us, answer us, and lead us
right to where He wants us to be.
God created us and has a plan for our lives that is just right for who we are, what we are good at, what we are interested in, and where we will thrive and work the best.

Date

Jesus asked him, "What do you want Me to do for you?"
"Lord, I want to see," he replied.
Luke 18:40–41

Just as Jesus answered and met his need when the blind man called out to Him, so Jesus is here today ready to hear our prayers and pleas for His help. Jesus is asking you right now, "What do you want Me to do for you?"

Date

From that time on Jesus began to preach,
"Repent, for the kingdom of heaven is near."
Matthew 4:17

This is Jesus' message, then and now: Change. To repent means to feel sorry for the wrongs you have done and to determine to change your mind and behavior. Dare to think of changing the way you approach life. God loves for people to change. It is rare, it is liberating, and it is Biblical.

Date

*A man with leprosy came and knelt before Him and said,
"Lord, if You are willing, You can make me clean." Jesus reached out
His hand and touched the man. "I am willing."*
Matthew 8:2–3a

Jesus is always ready to meet us right where we are today. He is never outdated.
He is not some old person whom you have to shelter from the "real world." He is prepared and ready to deal with all that is happening in our lives: the good, the bad, and even the unclean.
He is not afraid to touch us and lift us and get us going in the right direction again.
He is willing—take His hand and go His Way.

Date

Speak to one another with psalms, hymns and spiritual songs. Sing and make music in your heart to the Lord, always giving thanks to God the Father for everything, in the name of our Lord Jesus Christ.
Ephesians 5:19-20

Isn't it amazing
how singing a song of thanksgiving and praise
can make you feel so encouraged?

Date

My dear brothers, take note of this:
Everyone should be quick to listen, slow to speak and slow to become angry,
for man's anger does not bring about the righteous life that God desires.
James 1:19-20

This is such a daily discipline. The holding of the tongue must start with a resolve to hold it well before the opportunity presents itself.
Daily resolve to sift and filter thoughts to see if they even need to venture further than your mind (and then we still have to confess to idle and slanderous thinking)!
A constant challenge for believers!

Date

Whatever you do, work at it with all your heart,
as working for the Lord.
Colossians 3:23

We are called to be holy, compassionate, kind, humble, gentle, and forgiving. Of course we fall short, yet we must get up and start right back on the path with our Savior. We cannot afford to behave badly; our words and ways are a constant witness of Jesus and His presence in us.

Date

Rejoice in the Lord always.
I will say it again: Rejoice!
Philippians 4:4

Put rejoicing into your daily life: your prayer life, your music, your communication with others. Look for opportunities to rejoice and you will find them all around you—always.

Date

I pray also that the eyes of your heart may be enlightened
in order that you may know the hope to which He has called you,
the riches of His glorious inheritance in the saints, and
His incomparably great power for us who believe.
Ephesians 1:18-19a

Dear Heavenly Father, please let us see Your incomparably mighty power at work in our lives and our families' lives today. We acknowledge that You have protected us again and again; please protect us today so that Your plans will stand in our lives. Please bless us that we will see Your incomparably great power at work in our prayer lives for our faith and encouragement so that we will know how deep and wide Your love is for us.

In Jesus' name, Amen.

Date

And we know that in all things God works for the good of those who love Him, who have been called according to His purpose.
Romans 8:28

Everything God allows to happen in your life is permitted for a purpose—and that purpose is that we will become more like Jesus.

Date

*Then Jesus came to them and said, "All authority in heaven and on earth
has been given to Me. Therefore go and make disciples of all nations,
baptizing them in the name of the Father and of the Son and of the Holy Spirit,
and teaching them to obey everything I have commanded you.
And surely I am with you always, to the very end of the age."*
Matthew 28:18-20

Jesus is Lord and Master of everything now and forever.

Personal notes, favorite Scriptures, testimonies and praise reports, personal deliverance, prophetic dreams, visions, and revelations, etc.

The Gail Grace Nordskog Collection

Gail Grace Nordskog has been a passionate prayer journalist and intercessor for more than twenty-five years. She has found that

recording heartfelt emotions, prayers, and praise reports is a very intimate way of communing with God. As copublisher with her husband Jerry of Nordskog Publishing, she established the Gail Grace Nordskog Collection to produce inspirational and reflective prayer journals as companion pieces for selected books.

Upon reading Susie Hobson's powerful yet simple message in *Loving God with All Your Heart*, she knew that a prayer journal based on this message would be a perfect tool to help people grow in their love of God.

Gail hosts "Hearts of Promise," a television show encouraging Christians to seek God's will for their lives and to live out their lives with action and a passion for God and others. Many of her guests are missionaries who serve all over the world. Prior to this, Gail was the TV host of "A Message for Women." She also cohosted with Dr. Ted Baehr–founder and president of MovieGuide.org–his TV show, where she had the pleasure of interviewing the incredible Leigh Anne Tuohy (*The Blind Side*), and movie stars like Kirk Cameron (*Fireproof*) and Sandra Bullock (*The Blind Side*).

Gail is always seeking new ways to communicate through print and media the precepts and truth of God's Word in all areas of daily life. She has served on the board of an international adoption agency and as a branch director of the Ventura Office of Family Connections Christian Adoptions.

The Nordskogs live in Ventura, California, where Gail is a full-time wife and mother, spending the majority of her time raising their four school-age children who were adopted from China.

About the Author

Susie Hobson has a B.A. in Special Education and a master's degree in Rehabilitation Counseling from the University of Alabama. She worked as a rehabilitation counselor for the state Department of Rehabilitation Services for more than sixteen years, managing a deaf/hearing-impaired and blind/vision-impaired caseload. She retired five years ago to be a homemaker, spend more time with her family, and to write. She and her husband Rich have been married for more than twenty-nine years and live in Montgomery, Alabama. They have two daughters, Whitney and Amelia.

Susie has a profound sensory-neural hearing loss, which has prepared her to be the mother of their two daughters, both of whom are also hearing impaired. Whitney graduated from the University of Alabama majoring in journalism and political science and is pursuing a career as a conservative political journalist. Amelia, who painted the illustration on the front cover of the book, is studying art history. Both girls have a good, everyday relationship with the Lord. They know from Susie and Rich that there is an active spiritual world happening around them.

Rich earned his doctorate from the University of Alabama in Public Administration. In 2001, Chief Justice Roy Moore of the Alabama Supreme Court appointed him as director of the state court system. In 2003, when Chief Justice Moore was under attack for taking the stand to retain a monument in the courthouse honoring the Ten Commandments, Rich supported him and was fired after Judge Moore was removed from office. He is now Executive Director of the Foundation for Moral Law, a national non-profit law firm founded by Judge Moore that specializes in cases involving "the acknowledgment of God."

Rich and Susie are members of Lakeview Baptist Church, where they support the pro-life ministry as sidewalk counselors. Rich teaches the Young Married Couples Sunday-school class. He is also a deacon, the praise band leader, and a member of numerous Montgomery civic clubs.

Susie says, "My life is very full!"

To see all of our exciting titles and
view book contents, and to order ebooks
go to:
www.NordskogPublishing.com

If you like FREE information,
you are in for enjoyment, insight, and
inspiration via our **eNewsletter**.
Sign up here:
www.NordskogPublishing.com/eNewsletter

We also invite you to browse
many short articles, poems, and testimonies
by various perceptive writers.
To enjoy, go here:
www.PublishersCorner.NordskogPublishing.com

Ask your retailer or the publisher about
a discount when you purchase both
Loving God and the companion
Prayer Journal.

CONTACT THE PUBLISHER OR YOUR DISTRIBUTOR
FOR PUBLISHER DISCOUNT
ON THE TWO-BOOK SET
INCLUDING THE COMPANION BOOK
TO THIS PRAYER JOURNAL:
Loving God with All Your Heart:
Keeping the Greatest Commandment
in Everyday Life.

www.nordskogpublishing.com

Loving God Prayer Journal

$18.95
ISBN 978-0-9831957-2-6
51895>
9 780983 195726